Journey to th

A closer walk with God

By

Ayomide T Salau

Connect with Ayomide on

Facebook- Ayomide Salau

Instagram - ayomidesalau_rn

Twitter-   AyomideSalau_RN

LinkedIN- Ayomide Salau

You Tube- Ayomide Tolani Salau

Spotify and other music platform- ayosings

Blog- www.lifehealthandchristianity.com

All scripture quotes are taken from NLT and NKJV unless otherwise stated

Contents

Appreciation   5

Dedication   6

Introduction
 Prize giving day   8

Chapter One
 Reconciled   13

Chapter Two
The way that seems right   19

Chapter Three
 Come out from among them   24

Chapter Four
Can we be friends   28

Chapter Five
Why can't I   29

Chapter Six
 New wine in New wine skin   35

Chapter Seven
Living by the Spirit's power   40

Chapter eight
Closer too thee   44

Chapter nine
Intimacy with Christ   50

Chapter Ten
  Union with the Spirit   55

Chapter Eleven
I can move mountains   60

Chapter Twelve
  I have the Authority   69

Chapter Thirteen
  Go tell it on the mountain   75

Chapter Fourteen
  Workers in the vine yard   82

Chapter Fifteen
A bountiful Harvest   86

Appreciation

Dear Jesus,

Thank you for revealing yourself to me and taking me on a closer walk with you in your Vineyard. You are beautiful and awesome in all your ways and it is my desire that the whole world will come to know you.

Love always

Ayomide T Salau

Dedication

To all my beautiful friends who are in Christ Jesus or just about to meet him. I pray you have a divine encounter with the Lord as you read through this book.

Introduction

Prize giving day

I was recently reminded by the Holy Spirit of an event that happened when I was in Primary one. I was about Six years old at the time and due for promotion to primary two class. During Primary school, I was mostly awarded first, second or third position. The end of third term, always ended with Prize giving day. A day when Awards were being given to those who did excellently well in their classes. All the pupils from nursery one to primary six gathered on the assembly ground, including the teachers and headmistress.

The girls wore blue check gowns and blue berets, while the boys wore blue shorts, check buttoned shirts and blue face caps. This was the approved uniform for the school and everyone had to dress their best. It was the school rule for the girls to have same hair do and all pupils to wear brown covered shoes. Anyone found wanting with wrong hairdo or incomplete uniform was asked to stand out or kneel down as a form of punishment. It was pardonable if the pupil had a reasonable excuse for not having the correct hair do or complete set of uniform. On the day, we would listen to the long speech from the teachers and Headmistress. There was a popular assembly song that we often sang on the last day of the term.

Holiday is coming, Holiday is coming!
No more clanging bells
No more teachers' whip!
Goodbye teachers, Goodbye scholars
We are going on a jolly Holiday
Teacher : A jolly
Pupils : Holiday
Teacher : A jolly
Pupils: Holiday

This was a common Holiday song for many primary schools in Lagos, Nigeria. It was a reminder that we were free from the teachers' discipline, school regulations, early to rise, uniform routines, daily home works and all the hard work of primary school. Although we were going to miss our best friends and favourite teachers, everyone looked forward to the long Vacation. It was more exciting for those who had worked really hard during the term and were expecting awards.

Primary One A! The Headmistress announced.

First position - Ayomide Salau!

Second position - Amarachi!

Third Position-   Opeyemi!

I ran out with much excitement and stood on the podium waiting to receive my award. I received my prize from my class teacher and went home joyfully. On getting home, my nanny at the time noticed that it was written on it- Amarachi - second position. Oh dear! It was too late too change it. Everyone had gone home and school was over. I was not exactly sure if Amarachi went home with the prize for the first position or she went home with something else. One thing was certain, the teacher had handed over the wrong prizes to the right people.

Phillipians 3 :14 I press on to reach the end of the race and receive the heavenly prize for which God, through Christ Jesus, is calling us

There is always progression in life with everyone striving to win something or get to a higher level. Being awarded the appropriate prize for your labour is something that should bring joy and satisfaction. However, there is a higher calling than the schedules of life that keep us busy. Our calling is found in Christ Jesus which leads us to the prize of eternal life. In all our striving and hard work, we want to be on the right path that leads to God's vineyard. In his vineyard, there is a bountiful harvest and a reward for your labour. It requires a right relationship with God, Intimacy, Commitment, Faith, Knowledge of his will and reliance on the Holy Spirit to fulfil our divine calling. This has been made possible for us by the Crucifixion, Death and Resurrection of Christ Jesus. *His body and blood already paid the price for our eternal reward.*

On our e*ternal prize giving day*, there will be rejoicing for those who made it to the Vineyard. There will also be crying and wailing for those who do not meet the expectations of the award. We will receive our reward from the Peace of prince, Our Eternal Judge who rules with an Iron Sceptre. There will be a distinction between the Good and the Evil. The Good he will gladly welcome into his abode and the Evil he will say to them " I know you not". We can be rest assured that each one will be rewarded according to his labour and the right prizes will not be handed to the wrong people. Therefore, let us endeavour that we keep our eyes fixed on the PRIZE OF LIFE

It is worthy of note that our journey to the vineyard does not begin on the day of the prize giving. Just like the pupils who worked hard throughout the term, we are expected to be committed to our divine calling. In this Holy Spirit taught book, I will be sharing with you how we can take *A closer walk with God on our Journey to the vineyard.*

Chapter one
Reconciled

I used to live with my two siblings in Lagos, Nigeria, before I relocated to the United Kingdom three years ago. We lived together since childhood and were very fond of each other. The only time we were ever apart was when we had to return to boarding school or university after vacation. Other wise if we were to travel for holidays or go outing, it had to be the three of us going together. Between 2017 to 2019, I worked at the State Teaching hospital in Ikeja which was just about fifteen minutes drive from our house in Magodo G.R.A phase II.

I was only a few years into the nursing profession and faced with the challenges of a busy medical ward. Night shift was Sixteen hours long and we were often allocated one or two night duty per week. Going home famished in the Lagos hot weather after a busy night shift, I would stop at my favourite restaurant to get a plate of food. It was a popular Lagos *buka in* Ikeja. My order was mostly the same - *white rice and stew, beans, fried plantain, boiled egg, fish, cow skin* and a chilled can of *pepsi.* It was only about three hundred naira for a balanced diet, but well deserved. Sometimes, on getting home I would share the meal with my sisters or get an extra plate for them if they were around. They too had come too love the food as it was very tasty and rich in content.

One day I and my younger sister had a misunderstanding before I left for night shift and I did not apologise to her before leaving the house. While I was at work, I thought that the best way to *reconcile* with her was to get her my favourite *buka* meal as an *atonement offering.* So I got her an extra plate of food with a drink and handed it to her soon as I got home as a form of *offering* for reconciliation. She accepted it excitingly and that solved it. We were *reconciled* and got talking as usual.

Conflicts between people can lead to separation, while forgiveness brings about reconciliation. In the Old testament, God's children had to offer sacrifices of atonement for the forgiveness of sins and reconciliation. Sin from the beginning was what led to separation between God and man (Adam and Eve, Genesis chapter 3). Man was created to have fellowship with God but lost this relationship because of the sinful act they committed. This separation cost them a lot more than they could have ever imagined. Not only did they lose their peace with God, but lost access to their inheritance which was preserved for them in the Garden of Eden. Sin causes an everlasting separation between God and man, which means that anyone who does not repent from their sinful ways cannot receive the gift of eternal life.

Hebrews 9:9 For the gifts and sacrifices that the priests offer are not able to cleanse the consciences of the people who bring them.

In the book of Exodus 32, a similar occurrence is seen amongst the Israelites in the wilderness. They were given the old commandment as a guide to be in a right relationship with God, but were still carried away by worldly pleasures. On one occasion, they carved a golden calf as an idol for themselves even when God had instructed them not to worship false gods. They already forgot so soon how he delivered them with his mighty power out of slavery. Offering sacrifices of atonement for their sins was the only way for them to be reconciled with God. The High priests went into the Most Holy place of the tabernacle once a year to make atonement for them with the blood of goats and calves. The Israelites still did not have a perfect relationship with God, because this sacrifice was not an everlasting one and could not purify the minds of the people.

Romans 3: 23a For God presented Jesus as the sacrifice for sin. People are made right with God when they believe that Jesus sacrificed his life, shedding his blood.

In today's world a lot of people are still faced with the same separation that Adam and Eve encountered. They have no form of relationship with God because they are held bound by sin. It is God's will for all men to be reconciled to him and this has been made possible by the body and blood of Jesus Christ that was shed on the cross of Calvary. To be in right standing with God, we do not need to offer any atonement sacrifices with the *blood of goats and calves* like the High priests did for Israelites. If we simply confess our sins to God and ask him for forgiveness, he his able to forgive us and restore our relationship with him. By the *everlasting sacrifice* offered by Jesus our High priest, we now experience a perfect relationship with God.

Rev 5: 12 "Worthy is the Lamb who was slain

To receive power and riches and wisdom,

And strength and honour and glory and

blessing!"

Our Journey to the vineyard cannot begin without being in right standing with God. It is when we are reconciled that we can have a peaceful relationship with him. By the perfect blood of Jesus, we have everlasting freedom from sin, guilt and shame, and are made pure, holy and righteous before God our Father. When God is pleased with us he fills our hearts with his everlasting love. He is able to lead us on the path he has chosen for us. Also, we receive our divine Inheritance(Rev 5:12) which was purchased for us by Christ Jesus; who is the *Lamb that was slain* for our redemption.

If you have never given your life to Christ or not in right standing with God, you can say the simple prayer of salvation below before you proceed to the next chapters.

Dear Heavenly Father, I thank you for sending your only begotten son the Lord Jesus Christ to die for my sins on the cross of Calvary. I confess that I am a sinner and I ask that you cleanse me by the precious blood of Jesus that was shed for my redemption. I receive your love and forgiveness to be in right standing with you. I accept you into my life as my Father and I ask that you fill me with your Holy Spirit. I confess that Jesus is my Lord and I submit my life to you that you may lead me on this journey to the vineyard. Thank you Lord, In Jesus name. Amen.

Congratulations if you have just said this prayer, you are now in right standing with God. Welcome on board, seat belts on- It is a jolly ride to God's vineyard. I encourage you to join a bible believing church if you are not yet in one. You can ask God to lead you to one.

‘

Chapter Two

The way that seems right

Philosophy is one course I found quite interesting while I was in the University. Years after, I still remember one of the philosophical quotes we discussed in class. *" A straight stick in water appears bent'*. Various philosophers have analysed the meaning of this quote. My favourite analysis is Plato's ideology of virtual reality. For instance, when you hold the stick it feels straight and you can tell it is actually straight once you take it out of the water. When the straight stick is put back in water, we get an image of a bent stick. This appearance of the stick in water does not give us the reality of its true nature. One could easily conclude that the stick is bent if a proper analysis is not done. *It appears bent in water, but it is not.* Plato's analysis gives us an understanding on why people can be misled in certain circumstances. Your mind is presented with a vision that *seems right* but is *not exactly true.*

Proverbs 14:12 There is a path before each person that seems right, but it ends in death.

Many Christians have been misled into making decisions that are not in line with God's word. They hear the Good news and accept it, but somewhere along the line are misled by a false representation of the truth. Proverbs 14:12 warns us of the possibilities of taking the wrong turn in our Christian journey. People might often take the scriptures out of context to justify certain immoral acts. For instance, a Christian couple living together as unmarried partners may try to justify their sinful act. Possible humanly Justifications -*" We go to church on Sundays and attend regular bible studies", "We are both Christians and will eventually get married.","God is not concerned about our behaviour but sees our heart", " My parents were Christians but lived together before they got married".*

One very popular excuse is that the *Grace of God is sufficient for all,* therefore we can live freely. While it is true that we live by the grace of God, Romans 6 :1 begs the question - *Shall we continue in sin that grace may abound?* Certainly not. The grace of God is made available for us to live righteously and not to live according to the desires of the flesh.

Romans 12: 2 Don't copy the behaviour and customs of this world, but let God transform you into a new person by changing the way you think.

Absolute truth is that God's word cannot be compromised. There are no Scriptural justifications for unmarried Christian couples to live together in the same house. God does not allow it and still would not allow it, no matter how much society tends to make it fashionable. The bible clearly instruct us in Romans 12:2 not to copy the behaviour of the world, but allow God transform us into a new beings. Transformation of our minds happens by the word of God and the power of the Holy Spirit. Allowing God to renew our thoughts and attitude leads us in the path he has chosen for us. For this to happen we must give up the old sinful nature of the flesh and submit all our desires to Christ.

Genesis chapters 12 to 18 gives us an insight on how Abraham compromised God's word by taking the wrong path. God's promise to Abraham   was   to prosper him and make him a great nation. When Abraham arrived in Canaan, God appeared to him and promised to give the land to his descendants. God made this promise to him at the time when he had no children, though he and Sarah were married for several years. They were in their old age and it did not seem humanly possible that they could bear a child. Although Abraham believed God's promise, he still did not understand how this was going to be made possible. He could not fathom how he was going to be a great nation or how his descendants were to inherit the promised land. Abraham made a suggestion to the Lord that his servant will be his heir, but God did not approve of it. It was not going to happen the way Abraham thought it would, rather in the way God planned it from the beginning. Yet still, he went ahead to devise his own way of having a heir. He had intimate relations with Sarah's maid Hagar, who gave birth to Ishmael. To their amazement, God still did not approve of Ishmael as the heir.

Did God fulfil his promise of a heir to Abraham? Yes! Isaac was born fourteen years after Ishmael (Genesis chapter 21). Isaac was the heir God spoke about. God did not compromise his word just because Ishmael was born first. It *seemed right to* Abraham that engaging in an intimate relationship with Hagar was the way to have a heir. Perhaps if he waited a little longer and kept trusting the Lord, he might not have proceeded with his alternate plan. In the end, God was able to bring Abraham back to the pathway ordained for him.

Is it too late to turn around if you have wandered off from God's pathway for your life? NO! Nothing is ever too late for the Lord. He is able to correct any errors you might have made that has kept you far from the truth. Simply acknowledge your mistakes and come to him with a repentant heart. Submit all your desires to him and ask that he lead you on the path he has ordained for you.

Chapter Three
Come out from among them

In May 2021, I was led by the Holy Spirit to start my Blog-www.lifehealthandchristianity.com. The idea behind the blog was to write articles related to Life, Health and Christianity. One of my writing series was based on Friendship and Companionship. I studied, analysed and wrote on various kinds of friendship from the biblical perspective. This answered some of the questions that arose in my heart when I gave my life to Christ. Do we still remain in our old clique once we become born-again?. Can close companionship with unbelievers affect our walk with God?

2nd Corinthians 6:17

Therefore, come out from among unbelievers, and separate yourselves from them, says the LORD.

The first thing any new believer should do is to come out of any unholy association. Some believers persist too long in ungodly relationships or never find their way out of it. Again possible human excuses- "We went to high school together", "We are Childhood friends" "They helped me when I was an unbeliever", "I will lead them to Christ". It is right to lead them to Christ, but you need come out from that gathering and allow God transform you. I have often heard people say that they can keep going to the night club to preach to people. Some say God led them there to save others but use this as an excuse to keep clubbing and partying with unbelievers. Such a person is treading on a dangerous path and needs to reorder their steps in line with God's word. If your closest companions are unbelievers, you stand the chance of missing out on God's original plan for your life.

The book of Judges chapters 13 -16 tells us about Samson's consistent association with unbelievers and how he missed out on God's original plan for his life. Delilah, the woman he was fond of had ulterior motives and connived with the Philistines to capture him. Samson exposed the secret of his divine strength to her, which was his long hair. First, his fellowship with unbelievers, then Delilah shaving off his hair, and finally, him loosing all of his God-given strength. The next thing we see is Samson being captured by the philistines and thrown in prison. He suffered a great deal because he compromised God's word by keeping close association with unbelievers. Even though he was able to conquer them during their feast, that was not all God had for him. His divine calling was to begin to rescue the Israelites from the Philistines, but could not achieve this because he was caught up in the wrong association.

Are there still believers in similar circumstances like that of Samson? The friends in your circle do not see why you can no longer party with them all weekend. They are not happy that you stopped drinking alcohol or smoking with them either. Your partner does not understand why you chose purity over immorality. What is your bargain? To stay in the clique and keep convincing them about your decisions, or to submit totally to Christ and follow him on the Journey to the vineyard?. Or are you the "give to God what is God's and to Ceaser what is Ceaser's" type of believer? You can club all night on Fridays because it is fun and everyone is doing it and then on Sunday morning you are your best dressed in the front row in Church. Your best bet is to take the exit route from such association. Submit totally to Christ and let him take you on a closer walk with him.

Oh! We cannot isolate ourselves from unbelievers. Absolutely true, but you cannot also keep them as your close companions. Apostle Paul lets us know in 1st Corinthians 5:9 that we would have to leave the world to avoid unbelievers. So it is totally impossible not to have them around you. However, we are not to use this scripture as an excuse to remain in ungodly associations. How can we then show them love as the bible instructs us? You can pray for them while you are on your journey of faith. There is a reason why God chose you. You are *called out* for a purpose; to *stand out* and *lead* God's people. Practising what they practise will not help you or them either. They won't see the difference in you and certainly won't see any reason why they should accept Christ, if you still live the same way as they do. The best way to love them is to pray for their salvation. Living righteously and sharing the word with them will allow the light of God in you to shine over them.

Chapter four
Can we be friends?

Wait a minute! Did you pray about this? Do they share the same faith with you? Are they consistent in their walk with the Lord? Are they God's choice for you? Godly friends are not all about the "let's go for a holiday or let's go to the beach" kind of friends. They are friends that bring you closer to the Lord and encourage you to keep going in the direction that leads to God's vineyard. Can God bring such people to our lives? Yes! He's more than able. We are the body of Christ and should fellowship with other believers. This is the first step we take in forming Godly relationships once we become born-again.

Hebrews 10: 25 not forsaking our meeting together [as believers for worship and instruction], as is the habit of some, but encouraging one another; and all the more [faithfully] as you see the day [of Christ's return] approaching. AMP

While it is scriptural to attend Church gatherings and fellowship with other believers. It is also very important to discern with God's guidance when choosing close companions. For instance, in choosing a spouse or best friend, we cannot just choose any believer we come across in the church. As a matter of fact there are probably hundreds of Christians around you that might fit into your idea of a close companion. What makes the distinction is allowing God to bring the people he has chosen for you into your life. We see an example in Exodus 4:10-17 where God chose Aaron to be Moses's companion on his assignment. It is important to ask the Holy Spirit in prayer to lead you to your God ordained companion. Though the close companion might not come right after you become born-again, it is advisable to prayerfully wait on God. What you do not want to do at this point is to jump into the next available relationship. You might be missing out on God's best plan for your life.

Again, do we really need Godly friends? Oh well, the story of Daniel and his three friends answers this question (Daniel chapters 1-3). They were young Hebrew boys living in Babylon amongst people who served foreign gods. These young men were full of God's wisdom and refused to defile themselves. Despite all the threats issued by king Nebuchadnezzar, they were not compelled to worship the foreign gods. Did God come through for them! Yes! he certainly did. They experienced an outstanding miracle when they were thrown into the fiery furnace. The whole of Babylon stood still as they witnessed how God delivered them. They came out unhurt, without the slightest burn. I mean their clothes, hair, skin were perfectly intact. The God of Daniel, Shadrach, Meshach and Abednego proved his mighty wonders and his name was highly exalted in the whole of Babylon. A God like that, who wouldn't love him!

God ordained friendships are for us to make the Lord's name exalted in our lives and community. Daniel and his friends did not conform to the standards of society. They were the only ones in the entire city of Babylon who refused to worship the foreign god. Perhaps in your organisation, you might be the only one who does not attend the usual Friday night party with your colleagues after close of work. Suddenly you start contemplating - Oh well! Maybe I could just go for only one night, so they do not see me as a weird person. It's Friday night!- One glass of wine first! Oh not too bad, I will try another. Second glass! third! fourth! Oh, they are cheering you at this point. You are doing well! The next time they see you

you are consistent with five glasses or more every night and now an ambassador for alcoholic drinks.

Stop right there! Let's rewind a little! Before you make the decision to go for that Friday night party. Think! Is this in line with God's word? Is it beneficial to my soul? Are there other decent gatherings to attend? Remember who you are in Christ and know that God placed you in that organisation for a definite purpose. Do not let others compel you into making decisions that are not in line with God's word. Let your light so shine that others may see the good works of Christ in You (Matthew 5: 14- 16). Let others come to know Christ because of your obedience to him.

Chapter Five
Why Can't I ?

Slow down friend! Before you go on to say Jesus ate and drank with unbelievers, *why can't I*? Let us take a look at some instances from the bible when he did such. One instance is in Mark chapter two, when Levi accepted Jesus's call to be his disciple. He then invited him to his home for a feast along with other tax collectors and sinners. Levi was excited about his salvation which was why he invited all his friends to come and feast with Jesus. It was an opportunity for them to meet Christ and also receive their salvation. These people were termed unworthy by the Pharisees. Jesus's response to them was that he had come to save the unrighteous and not those who think they are righteous.

Luke chapter 19 gives us another instance of Zacchaeus who was a wealthy chief tax collector. He was really wanted to see Jesus, but had to climb a tree because of height. When Jesus cited him, he called him to come down quickly and agreed to have dinner with him. The people were displeased with this , but Jesus's response again was that he came for those who were lost. It is important to highlight that Zacchaeus really wanted to know Christ and his immediate response was to joyfully accept him in his home. He repented out-rightly and received his salvation.

Simon the Pharisee in Luke chapter 7 is also another person who invited Jesus to his home. A certain woman who heard Jesus was around came to the house. She wept at his feet, wiped them with her hair and anointed them with alabaster perfume. Jesus had compassion and forgave her because of her repentant heart. Simon and his friends were distraught that Jesus would engage with a sinner. Jesus did not encourage such attitude but chastised them for their unrepentant heart. Jesus was in their home, but they missed their salvation because their hearts were hardened.

Have you told your friends about Jesus yet?. Jesus entertained sinners because he had compassion on them. It was because of our sins that he gave himself on the cross of Calvary. He was never in the act of conforming to worldly standards, but went about doing good, preaching to the people, healing the sick and setting the oppressed free. He just concluded a forty day and forty night fast in the wilderness before he selected his disciples. These were the people whom Christ spent most of his time with, teaching and revealing to them the secrets of God's kingdom. Their divine purpose was to help him fulfil his ministry on earth and to carry on doing the good works even after his ascension. The relationship between Christ and his disciples is worthy of emulation. Before you join that association or ask someone to join yours, you must prayerfully discern if they are in God's plan for your life. If you are uncertain about your relationships, simply ask the Lord in prayer to reveal to you if you are in the right association You have been completely set free, so do not get yourself tangled up in ungodly relationships (Galatians 5:1).

Chapter Six
New wine in new wine skin

The memory of the blue and red checkers come to my mind in this chapter. Blue checkers! Run down here! the seniors would call. This was the time when you had to make a swift decision. It was either you were running towards the senior, running away from them or sprinting past them *-if you were bold enough*. Running humbly towards the seniors was a huge price to pay. Chances are you would be taken into the senior dormitory (dorm) and once you are in there, you become *a sacrificial lamb ready to be slain*. There was always a long list of manual labour in the senior dorm and you would most likely be turned into that errand Junior girl in blue check. Your best bet would have been to sprint past them. Junior girls usually walked in groups when they were going past the senior dorm. So it was always fun to run past the senior girls when they started calling- J girls come here! Blue checkers! All of you come here!.

I attended an All Girls boarding school in Benin city, Nigeria between 2002-2007. Classes usually ended at 2.30 pm and then everyone would go to the dining hall for lunch. It was after lunch that you get to change into your house wear and go about your usual afternoon routines. One thing that was almost impossible was to hide your identity. The blue check or red check was your identity. Wearing a blue check house wear at that time meant that you were a Junior girl (J girl) from JSS1 to JSS3, while the red check house wear was for senior girls from SS1 to SS3. If you desired a change of identity, it meant you had to pass your exams and graduate from Junior school. The change of identity becomes visible when you are promoted to senior school. You no longer identify as a blue checker but now a red checker living in the senior dorm.

The book of Acts chapter 7 and 8 tells us about Saul's persecution of the church and his conversion to Christianity. He was one of those present at the martyr of Stephen, an apostle of Christ. After the death of Stephen (martyred for his belief in Christ), there was a wave of persecution amongst the Christians. Saul was notorious for the persecution of the believers at that time. He went about destroying churches and arresting Christians. He encountered Jesus on his way to Damascus, which was what led to his conversion. He received a change of identity after this encounter and the old Saul was no longer visible. Paul (former Saul) then became known for preaching the gospel and performing miracles in Jesus's name. His Identity in Christ is what everyone could now see and partake in. He now lived amongst the believers and fellowshipped with them.

Paul was called and chosen for great works of the kingdom just like you and I. Once he accepted this call, the old ways of persecuting Christians had to go. Such behaviour did no longer fit into his new calling in Christ. He had to repent, get baptised and begin a new life in Christ Jesus. It was after his conversion that he began to fulfil his divine purpose which was to take the message of the Gospel to the Gentiles, Kings and people of Israel.

Mark 2:22 "And no one puts new wine into old wineskins. For the wine would burst the wineskins, and the wine and the skins would both be lost. New wine calls for new wineskins."

In Mark chapter 2, the people were bothered because Jesus's disciples were not fasting along with the disciples of John the baptist and the Pharisees. They were instead spending most of their time with Jesus. This wasn't to say that fasting was not required of his own disciples, but they did not have to conform to the behaviour of others. Our new life in Christ means that we have a new identity which is completely different from the old. The old or regular ways of society won't fit in our new life, just like the old wine won't fit in a new wine skin. Jesus's disciples didn't fit either in the regular ways of the other disciples. They had encountered Christ and therefore had to live like him.

Ephesians 4: 21 -24 Since you have heard about Jesus and have learned the truth that comes from him, throw off your old sinful nature and your former way of life, which is corrupted by lust and deception. Instead, let the Spirit renew your thoughts and attitudes. Put on your new nature, created to be like God—truly righteous and holy.

In the same way, once we encounter Christ and have knowledge of him, we are no longer bound by the old sinful nature because it has been nailed to the cross at crucifixion. We are to get rid of the old nature of sin that leads to death and put on our new nature of righteousness which leads to eternal life. God expects us to live a righteous and holy life because we have been given the power to do so at salvation. Just like the disciples spent most of their time with Christ and learnt Godly ways of living. We are encouraged to commune daily with Christ through prayer and study of the word. The word of God is Jesus as revealed in John 1:1 and has the power to transform us into new beings. The more we study the word, the more we have a revelation of who Jesus is and this way we can live like him.

Dear friend, do not forget who you are. A new creation in Christ Jesus! *A new wine in new wine skin!* It's time to say good bye to the old ways. Everything has become new in your life, so live a life of holiness- *a life that pleases Jesus.*

Chapter seven
Living by the Spirit's power

Acts 1 :8 But you will receive power when the Holy Spirit comes upon you.

The disciples first had an encounter with the Holy Spirit when they were in the upper room praying. Jesus had told them to wait on him before they could go out to preach the gospel. He told them that they will receive power once they were baptised with the Holy Spirit. It was after the baptism of the Holy Spirit that they were able to carry out the greats works of the kingdom of God. They were able to speak in other tongues, testify of the gospel and perform miracles.

It was on this same day of pentecost that 3000 people were saved and added to the church, after Peter had preached the gospel. Peter was able to testify of the kingdom of God , because he was filled that day with the Spirit of Boldness. When we are filled with the Holy Spirit and choose to follow his leading in every part of our lives, we become more than conquerors and are able to live a supernatural Christian life.

Galatians 5: 16 So I say, let the Holy Spirit guide your lives. Then you won't be doing what your sinful nature craves.

19 -21 When you follow the desires of your sinful nature, the results are very clear: sexual immorality, impurity, lustful pleasures, idolatry, sorcery, hostility, quarrelling, jealousy, outbursts of anger, selfish ambition, dissension, division, envy, drunkenness, wild parties, and other sins like these.

22-23 But the Holy Spirit produces this kind of fruit in our lives: love, joy, peace, patience, kindness, goodness, faithfulness, gentleness, and self-control. There is no law against these things.

Our thoughts and attitudes are being transformed by the power of the Holy Spirit. Once we become born-again, we receive the Holy Spirit who begins to dwell in us. He is in union with our spirit and our body his temple. He fills us with his power and also gives the ability to overcome the sinful nature of the flesh. We are no longer led by the desires of the flesh once we submit ourselves to him. He fills us with the Fruits of the Spirit that enables us live an abundant life pleasing to God. It is important that we acknowledge his presence in our lives and fellowship more with him through prayer and worship. If you have never had an encounter with him before or you are not sure, simply ask him to fill you with his presence. You can also ask him for a fresh encounter with him as you go along on your journey to the vineyard.

If you have never being received a baptism of the Holy Spirit before with the evidence of Speaking in tongues. Simply say the prayer below:

Dear Holy Spirit, I thank you for the love that you have for me as a believer. I ask that you come into my life and fill me with your presence and power. I submit myself to you and ask that you guide and lead me in my walk with God. I accept you into my life and I choose this day to walk closely with you as my friend and lover. Thank you for filling me with your presence and power. In Jesus name, Amen.

Congratulations, you are filled with the Holy Spirit and can now commune with him. You have also received the gift of speaking in tongues, so begin to speak with faith. Endeavour to follow his leading in every part of your life.

Chapter eight
Closer to thee

Lord there is a longing only you can fill
A raging tempest only you can still
My soul is thirsting for you oh my God
Lord quench my thirst
Lord feed my soul

Take me deeper in love with you
Jesus take me deeper in love
Hold me closer in love with you
Jesus hold me closer in love with you

In your love is found great faithfulness
Your love is filled with hope and peace
Your love is filled with compassion and love
Oh teach me Lord to love thee back

Yes from sunrise to sunrise I seek your face
From day to day I long for your touch
To hold my hand Lord lest I fall
To draw me nearer closer to thee

Deeper in love was one of my favourite hymns growing up in the Orthodox church. Once the Choir began to sing, it was as if the floodgates of heaven had opened on us. I could sense an intimate desire to just keep loving the Lord, even though I had not met him personally yet until I became born-again. After mass I would carry on singing this song passionately over and over again all day. I remembered this hymn recently and took a closer look at the lyrics. It made me realise how much we all need the love of Christ. The Hymn talks about how much our soul thirsts for the Lord and the need for him to quench this desire with his love. I encourage you to listen to the audio if you have never heard it before.

John 4 13- 14 Jesus replied, "Anyone who drinks this water will soon become thirsty again. But those who drink the water I give will never be thirsty again. It becomes a fresh, bubbling spring within them, giving them eternal life."

John 4 : 1- 42 tells us the story of the Samaritan woman who had come to the well to draw water and encountered Jesus. This woman was known to have had five husbands in the past and was not presently living with any of them. None of the five husbands were able to satisfy the longings of her heart. It was obvious from her story that she was yearning for something she still had not found. On this fateful day she encountered Christ and her thirst was quenched.

John 4:7b Jesus said to her, "Please give me a drink

When Jesus asked her for a drink, she was amazed that a Jew could ask a Samaritan for anything. This was because the Jews seldom relate with the Samaritans. Fortunately, she had just met with a different kind of Jew. The kind of Jew who wasn't bound by race, colour, sex, social class and all the other classifications that segregate people in the society. Asking her for a drink meant *" Hey, I see you, we can talk, I'm right here" "you can come closer"*. It was an invitation for a closer relationship, which was more than just saying *hello* by the well and going home afterwards.

John 4:26 Then Jesus told her, "I AM the Messiah!"

Jesus was far reaching and wanted more than just the initial conversation. He began to reveal himself to her gradually and made her realise that in him, she would have eternal life. He was the one she had been searching for and the only one who could satisfy that longing in her soul. The water from the well wasn't going to do justice to that, neither would getting married to husband number six.

The Samaritan woman was honest in her reply. She said, "I have no husband" when Jesus asked her to "Go get her husband" because she wasn't living with anyone of them at the moment. She had heard about the messiah and had been longing to meet him. She was expectant and believed that meeting him will bring answers to all her questions. Look who was right there in front of her! The Messiah! Her immediate reaction was to run to her town and announce to everyone that she had met the Messiah. She came back to Jesus with her entire neighbourhood so that they could also meet him.

John 4: 6b Jesus, tired from the long walk, sat wearily beside the well about noontime.

Jesus was already at the well that day waiting for her. It wasn't a coincidence, he knew she was going to be there that day. Jesus knew everything about her and how much she had longed to meet him. He was waiting to give her redemption for her soul and lead her to *God's vineyard.* Jesus is always willing to nourish our souls if only we open up our hearts in response to him. Being honest in our relationship with him will also lead us to greater depths of his love, just like the Samaritan woman encountered.

Psalm 23: 2b, 3a He leads me beside the still waters. He restores my soul;

Have you met with him! I'm not talking about the going to church every Sunday kind of meeting with the Lord. I am talking about a genuine encounter with Christ that brings about restoration for our souls. Sometimes people get too busy to spend time in his presence. This could be work related, family issues or maybe just the usual things of life that keep us busy. Our relationship with Christ should be our topmost priority on a daily basis. We need to set aside time each day to just to be in the quietness of his presence and be intimate with him. You could do this during your break at work, during train or bus travels, early in the morning or at night time away from everyone else. Shut your mind to all the worries of life and just connect with the *Prince of peace*. There is no perfect place or time to encounter the Lord, just be willing to respond to his love.

Psalm 46: 10 Be still, and know that I am God;

Through worship, prayer and study of the word we get closer to the Lord. It is not okay to hurriedly read a few verses of the bible, sing one worship song, mumble a few prayer points, pack your bags and that's it for the day. Don't be so concerned either about all the issues you have to pray about. Just like he knew the Samaritan woman, he knows you too well. He is very much aware of all your heart desires and would grant them according to his will. God is Omnipotent, Omnipresent and Omniscient. He is in control of that situation, just be still in his presence and allow his glory radiate all over you.

Chapter Nine
Intimacy with Christ

Intimacy with the Christ brings us to a deeper revelation of his glory. Jesus had twelve disciples and several other followers, but only three of them had an intimate relationship with him. Peter, James and John were his intimate disciples and were the ones whom Jesus went with whenever he needed some alone time. With these three, he revealed more of himself than he did with the other disciples.

Mark 6: 46 After telling everyone good-bye, he went up into the hills by himself to pray.

We can learn from Jesus how to be intimate with God. He often went away from the crowd just to be with his Father. It was a period when he desired that peaceful quietness, away from the issues of life to just to commune with God. One of such instance was when he went alone to the wilderness to fast and pray for forty days and nights before he began his ministry (Luke 4:1-15). Another instance was when he sent the multitude away and told the disciples to go ahead of him to Bethsaida (Mark 6:45-47). He had just catered for five thousand people and needed to have some alone time (Mark 6:30-44). These were times when he was not concerned about the crowd or the disciples, but prioritised his relationship with God.

There are two significant events in the life of Jesus when only his Intimate friends had to be present. The first was at the transfiguration when his Glory was revealed to them (Mark 9 :2-12). They had gone up to pray with him suddenly, *his appearance was transformed, his face shone like sun and his clothes became white as light (Vs 2 & 3).* He was seen talking with Moses and Elijah and as soon as the cloud overshadowed him, they heard a voice saying *this is my dearly beloved son who brings me great joy, Listen to him (Vs 7).* Jesus's Glory as the son of God had just been revealed to them and he clearly instructed them not to tell anyone about it until his resurrection. They were the only ones amongst the disciples whom Jesus revealed himself to in this manner.

Earlier in Mark 8: 27- 30, Peter testified that Jesus is the Son of the Living God. Jesus in response acknowledged that only his Father in heaven could have revealed this to Peter. It was not for the ordinary mind to know but only those who had a revelation of him. It was after this encounter that Jesus began to reveal more about his death and resurrection to his other disciples. The more intimate we are with Christ, the more we have a revelation of who he is.

Mark 14:37 b Couldn't you watch with me even one hour

The second significant event was at the garden of Gethsemane (Mark 14: 32-42) with his disciples. Jesus took with him Peter, James and John to keep watch while he prayed. This was the event before the crucifixion and he was deeply troubled. While in the garden, Jesus prompted his intimate friends twice to keep watch with him even for one hour. He wanted them to share in his suffering, but they had fallen asleep. At the time before he was arrested, Jesus gave them the revelation that the hour had come for him to be handed over to his betrayers. This was a significant time in his life that only his intimate disciples were aware of. Will you keep watch with him even for one hour? Are you willing to share in his suffering? His intimate disciples were there with him to share in his glory at the transfiguration and also in his suffering before crucifixion.

Being an intimate friend of Christ means that you will be entrusted with greater works for God's vineyard. In Mark chapter 5 (21-23, 35-43), Jairus the Synagogue leader informed Jesus that his daughter was very sick and wanted him to come to his house to heal her. While Jesus was yet on his way, people from Jairus's home came to inform him that the young girl had passed way. Jesus, knowing that the girl was still alive went ahead to their house. On getting there, He went inside the girl's room with only Peter, James, John and her parents . He didn't let anyone else go in with him to witness what he was going to do.

When they were all present in the room and everyone else had gone out, Jesus held the girl's hand and asked her to get up. Immediately she got up and began walking around. This was one of the events accounted for in the bible where Jesus raised the dead. Only those who were close to him were entrusted with this great miracle that happened. Again, being intimate with Christ means that he can trust us with even greater works for God's kingdom. Are you willing to be entrusted with greater works in God's vineyard?

Are you one of his intimate friends? Our walk with God requires deeper levels of intimacy. Jesus desires a loving relationship with us and not a religious one. Don't just love him from a distance by marking your attendance in Church and prayer meetings. Get closer to him and commune with him daily in the stillness of his presence. While we sit quietly in his presence, we get acquainted with his Spirit and are able to discern his voice. He is able to heal our hearts , fill us with his love and teach us his ways. It is only when you are intimate with Christ that you can share in his Glory.

Chapter Ten
Union with the Spirit

Often times we hear people deliberate on how human beings were created. There are several scientific facts in evolutionary biology on the origin of human species. One of the topics I found quite interesting during Social studies classes in Junior secondary school, was the evolution of man from the Hominid category. The earliest hominids *Homo habilis* and *Homo erectus* originated from Sub Saharan Africa and had specific characteristics like other Primates such as chimpanzees.

Homo habilis existed nearly over 1,5 to 2,4 million years ago and were said to have gone into extinction as a result of climate change. The modern man today is classified as *Homo sapiens* which were said to have evolved from *Homo erectus* over 200, 000 to 300,000 years ago. All other classification of the Hominids have long gone into extinctions.

Genesis 1:26 Then God said, "Let Us make man in Our image, according to Our likeness.

In Genesis chapter one we see a true story of creation and the origin of man. Genesis 1:2 tells us that the *Spirit of God was hovering over the waters* in the beginning. Creation began from the word spoken by God when he said *Let there be.* The earth was without form and void, which meant that there was nothing in existence. There was no light , no animals, trees or even human beings at that time. The world began to evolve when God (The Father) spoke the *Word* (Jesus) into existence by the Holy Spirit (Spirit of God). The *Word (Jesus)* that he spoke was life and set the world in motion (John 1: 4). Man was created from this very *Word* of God (Jesus) that was spoken in the beginning (John 1:3). From this we understand that human beings came into existence through God who was there from the very beginning (John 1:1). Man was created peculiarly in the image and likeness of God, which means we are Spirit beings like our Father in heaven (Genesis 1: 27).

In the beginning, we see how God worked in harmony to bring creation into existence, which reminds us of the

Trinity (Three persons in one God, God the Father, God the Son and God the Holy Spirit). In this chapter, we will be focusing more on the third person of the Trinity which is the Holy Spirit. Our first revelation of the Holy Spirit is in Genesis 1:2 which means *He Was* even before the foundation of the world and still *Is* with us today and for all ages to come. From time to time he has been with man, guiding and leading us through the Journey to the vineyard.

Romans 8:16 For his Spirit joins with our spirit to affirm that we are God's children.

Moses was to lead the Israelites on the Journey out of *Egypt* through the *wilderness* to the *Promised land.* For him to successfully lead them, he had to be in close communion with God through the Holy spirit. On one occasion he stayed 40 days and 40 nights in God's presence on Mount Sinai, before the tablets of the covenant law was handed to him (Laws to enable the Israelites live righteously, Exodus 34) . In this period, he ate no food nor drank water, but was on the mountain just communing with the Lord. The Spirit of God is in union with our Spirit and able to lead us in every area of our lives. *(Romans 8:16).* He is our Eternal guide for all ages to come and only through close fellowship with him can we journey to God's vineyard. He speaks to us in various ways through our minds, the Word, dreams, visions or through another believer. When we take time out to be in God's presence, we are able to discern the guidance of the Holy Spirit .

Acts 10:19-20 While Peter thought about the vision, the Spirit said to him, "Behold, three men are seeking you. Arise therefore, go down and go with them, doubting nothing; for I have sent them."

Guidance through the Holy Spirit not only makes an impact in our lives, but in the lives of others around us. God's will is for all men to be saved and when we are led by the Holy Spirit in our ministry, we are able to bring others into the body of Christ. Peter was one of the disciples who received the baptism of the Holy Spirit on the day of Pentecost and preached the gospel that led to the salvation of 3,000 men in one day (Acts chapter 1). In Acts chapter 10 Peter had a vision and was instructed by the Holy Spirit to follow the three men that were seeking him. He did not assume any doubts in his heart but was very certain that the word he received was from the Holy Spirit. He simply obeyed the instruction that was given to him and followed the men who had come from Cornelius' house. All those whom Peter preached to that day in Cornelius' house received their salvation and were baptised.

Philip was another close disciple of Christ who followed the leading of the Holy Spirit. In Acts chapter 8, Philip was led to the desert by an Angel of the Lord. On reaching there, the Holy Spirit instructed him saying *"Go near and overtake this chariot."* (Acts 8:29). The man in the Chariot happened to be a Ethiopian Eunuch who had gone to Jerusalem to worship and was trying to understand the scriptures. Philip immediately followed the instructions of the Holy Spirit and got in the Chariot with him. By this, he was able to preach to the Eunuch which led to his repentance and baptism by water.

Communion, discernment and obedience are three key steps in following the guidance of the Holy Spirit. Moses, Peter and Philip are some examples of God's chosen people in the bible who were able to fulfil their divine purpose and impact the lives of many. They committed their time to knowing the Lord, which was why they were able to discern his voice and follow his leading. On our *Journey to the Vineyard,* we must ensure close fellowship with the Holy Spirit through prayer, fasting, worship and study of the word. In-depth study of the word helps us to discern his voice and know his leading. The Holy Spirit will not lead us in anyway contrary to the word of God. *He is the Spirit of truth* and leads us into all truth (John 14:16). As we begin to trust and obey him, then we can successfully fulfil our divine purpose here on earth.

Chapter Eleven
I can move mountains

Those who studied geography in school probably learnt a lot about mountains. It wasn't really one of my favourite subjects in secondary school and I had to drop the subject after the first term. Gratefully it wasn't compulsory for Science students to offer the subject. Anyway, I still know a thing or two about mountains and I know for sure that they are fixed in certain locations with high altitudes far above sea levels. For instance, mount Everest known as the highest mountain is located in China and Nepal and is about 29,035 feet (8,850 meters). Mount Wycheproof is known as the smallest mountain, located in Australia and only about 486 feet (148 meters) above sea levels.

Mountains are large masses of rocks and soil formed from the earth's tectonic plates smashing together. People who have gone mountain hiking would have had a closer feel of what substance it is made of and how difficult it is to climb one. I am not certain I would be adding mountain Hiking to my list of life adventures, but I do know for sure that *I can move mountains.*

One might wonder, how can I move mountains? I mean they are tall, large hard rocks and don't seem like their locations could change either. I mean mount Everest hasn't moved from where it was since the world began. So why does Jesus tell us in Matthew 17: 20 *we can move mountains*. We know that God created mountains, so why is he asking us to move them? Can Jesus help us move these mountains? What kind of mountain is Jesus expecting us to move? What is the possibility that I can actually move one? What do I need to move one?

Firstly, we need to establish that Jesus did use a lot of parables to teach the people. After he taught the crowd on some occasions, he did explain the meaning of the parables to the disciples. The disciples wondered why Jesus taught others with parables and not them. His response to this was that they *are permitted to understand the secrets of the Kingdom of Heaven, but others are not* (Matthew 13 :11). As friends of Jesus, we have the ability to understand the word of God by revelation from the Holy Spirit. Jesus did make it plain to those who listened to his teaching, *more understanding will be given, and they will have an abundance of knowledge (*Matthew 13 :12).

His disciples usually met with him privately so he could teach them the meaning of the parables. Meaning that as we dedicate more time to studying the word daily we receive a divine revelation of who Jesus is. John 1:1 tells us that Jesus is the Word. Therefore, studying the bible regularly means we are getting to know him. It is important to set time out daily to study the bible chapter by chapter. Reading only a few verses a day won't help you in your spiritual growth or your knowledge of Christ. If you are a new believer, you can start by studying one chapter of the new testament daily, asking the Holy Spirit for divine understanding and revelation the word. For maturing believers I recommend getting a bible plan or devotional that helps you complete the bible within one to two years.

Matthew 17: 20 "You don't have enough faith," Jesus told them. "I tell you the truth, if you had faith even as small as a mustard seed, you could say to this mountain, 'Move from here to there,' and it would move. Nothing would be impossible."

Jesus uses this Scripture in Matthew 17: 20 to illustrate to his disciples the kind of faith that was required to perform miracles. The mountain in this context referred to the nature of the circumstances they were expected to change. To a Geographer, a mountain might seem totally impossible to move or be moved. Spiritually, those mountains Jesus quoted here are circumstances that people might encounter in their daily lives. With an *ordinary mindset,* it might seem impossible for those circumstances to change or turn around. Being that *we have the mind of Christ* (1st Corinthians 2:16b), we are able to turn around any situation when we put our faith to work.

The disciples encountered a man whose son was possessed by an evil spirit but they could not cast it out. The man approached Jesus and reported that the disciples had prayed for his son but could not heal him. Jesus chastised them in regards to their faith and went ahead to heal the boy. Later on, they met him privately because they were concerned on why they could not perform the miracle. Jesus revealed to them that their faith was not enough to cast out the evil spirit. On this occasion they couldn't seem to put their faith to work because they possibly had doubts in their hearts.

Fear is usually a major challenge to the faith of many Christians. In Matthew 14 (22-32), the disciples were across the land away from Jesus and there was a strong wind blowing. Soon they looked up and saw Jesus walking on water towards them. They where terrified and thought they had seen a ghost. A conversation ensued afterwards between Jesus , his disciples and Peter.

Disciples: *"It's a ghost!"*
Jesus: Take courage, I am here
Peter : Lord, if it's really you, tell me to come to you, walking on the water
Jesus: "Yes, come," Jesus said.

In this conversation we can see two attributes portrayed by the disciples. The first was that of fear, when they thought they had seen a ghost. The second was a change in Peter's attitude once Jesus calmed their fears. Peter became bold enough to speak and asked the Lord to tell him to walk on water, if he was really the one. He began to trust that it was the Lord speaking to him. Peter was an intimate disciple of Christ and knew that he could totally trust him. He knew that Jesus wasn't going to ask him not to take those steps of Faith. Jesus strengthened his faith by asking him to take those bold steps. One major lesson here is that we need to overcome our fears for our faith to work. We also need to trust the Lord enough that he will give us the right instructions just when we need it. In our walk with him, we are expected to follow his guidance in taking bold steps of faith that enable us walk on stormy waters.

On this same occasion, we see a turn of event once Peter started walking on water. A second conversation ensued between Jesus and Peter.

Peter: "Save me, Lord!" he shouted.
Jesus: "You have so little faith," Jesus said. "Why did you doubt me?"

This time around Peter was terrified by the strong winds and began to sink. Fear became a major challenge to Peter's faith and the resultant effect was him sinking in water. Peter was taken aback by the waves that he no longer thought he could walk on water. This was the same person who earlier took those bold steps of faith, but surprisingly began to doubt once he realised the situation was beyond him. In reality, Jesus knew that

Peter was able to overcome that situation to get to him. Peter on the other hand became concerned about the turbulent waves, rather than walking towards Jesus. He was able to rise above the waves because Jesus reached out to him, held his hand and led him safely to the boat. Peter still trusted in the Lord, which was why he called out to him. Though overwhelmed by the situation, he still believed that Jesus was able to reach for him. He trusted that calling on Jesus would get him out of that turbulent situation. We are encouraged to look beyond the challenges that we might encounter in our walk with God and keep trusting the Lord. Even though we might feel overwhelmed at some point, we should always keep in mind that Jesus is able to uplift us above the waters. It is important that we call out to him in those difficult situations.

We can learn from this scenario with Jesus , Peter and his other disciples, that one important way to put our faith to work is to trust in the Lord. The word of God sharpens our faith and we need to hold on to every word that he has said about us. In the bible we can find a lot of promises that God has spoken regarding our inheritance in Christ Jesus. *I am a Child of God Romans 8:16, I am*

God's workmanship Ephesians 2:10, I can do all things through Christ who strengthens me Phillipians 4:13 , I am more than a conqueror through Christ who loves me Romans 8:37, I am the light of the world Matthew 5: 14, I am redeemed by the blood of Jesus 1st Peter 1 : 18-19. These scriptures are reminders of who we are in Christ Jesus. In our journey to God's vineyard, we might encounter situations that would test our faith. When faced with such situations, it is important that we keep proclaiming the word of God. It's not the time to question our faith or succumb to fear. It's the time to keep trusting in the lord and remember that n*othing is impossible to those who believe* (Mark 9:23).

Chapter Twelve
I have the Authority

I used to watch a lot of NOLLYWOOD epic movies on African magic when I was much younger - *before I became Born-again.* I loved watching the ones that portrayed the Igbo culture. I loved absolutely everything about the attire, the make-up, the music, food, dance, drinks and so much more. One thing I found quite interesting was the use of the *Staff (Ofo)* as a symbol of *authority and truth.* The *Ofo* was usually in possession of the eldest person in a clan or community.

The *Ofo* holder possessed special rights and privileges granted to him by the *gods.* The people were under his guidance and were expected to report matters to him because of his spiritual authority. He was able to resolve their conflicts, protect and intercede for them. In some cases, if the *Ofo* was stolen from the land, the people were exposed to danger and possible invasion by their enemies. There was no form of protection over them because the symbol of authority was missing. They had to seek ways to recover the *Ofo,* so they could continue living peacefully. I am grateful that as a believer, I am no longer bound by any form of traditional supremacy, because *I have the Authority* in Christ Jesus.

Exodus 4: 20b In his hand he carried the staff of God.

Moses was an exceptional leader because he carried the *Staff of God* in his hand. The staff was a symbol of *divine authority* given to him by God to perform mighty miracles and bring the Israelites out from captivity. Until he had his first encounter with God at mount Sinai, the staff was only a shepherd's staff. It was when he answered the call of God that it became the *Staff of God.* Moses witnessed what the *Staff* was able to do when he was up on the mount. He was convinced that he had the authority and could perform miracles with it. When he approached Pharaoh, he did exactly as God instructed him and all the miracles came to pass.

Moses performed several miracles with the Staff of God in hand as recorded throughout the book of Exodus. When the Israelites were about to cross the Red sea, Moses stretched out his staff over the sea and parted the waters for them to walk on dry ground. Another occasion when the people were thirsty on their journey and had no water to drink, God instructed him to strike the rock with his staff. He did exactly as he was told and water came gushing out of the rock One time when the Israelites were engaged in a battle with the Amalekites, Moses went to the top of the hill and held up the *Staff of God.* Anytime he held up the staff the people of Israel were on the winning side, but anytime he held it down the Amalekites were winning. The Israelites won the battle because of Moses's persistence in holding the staff up. Moses and his people were victorious because they had the divine authority of the Lord. (Exodus chapters 14 &17).

Matthew 16:19 And I will give you the keys of the kingdom of heaven, and whatever you bind on earth will be bound in heaven, and whatever you loose on earth will be loosed in heaven."

Once we encounter Christ and answer his call upon our lives, we receive the Keys of the Kingdom of heaven. These words were first spoken to Peter when he had a divine revelation of Christ. Only when we have a divine revelation of Jesus, can we then know the relevance of the authority we possess. The Keys are a significance of the divine authority that Christ has given us, with which we can lock and unlock any Spiritual doors. We have divine access to the kingdom of heaven and have been given the authority to bring it down to earth. With these keys we can release supernatural miracles from the throne of God through our worship and prayers. When we make prophetic declarations with the word of God we experience a manifestation of God's power in our lives and ministry.

Luke 10 :19 Behold, I give you the authority to trample on serpents and scorpions, and over all the power of the enemy, and nothing shall by any means hurt you

With our divine authority, we are able to perform miracles in the name of Jesus. When Jesus first sent the seventy-two disciples out, they returned joyfully and testified that even the demons submitted to them in his name. We have been given the power to heal the sick, proclaim the word, cast out evil spirits, raise the dead and set the oppressed free in the name of Jesus. The higher we go in our walk with God, the more power he releases to us.

Peter, Paul and Silas are great examples of disciples in the bible who had the divine authority of Christ and were able to set many free from oppression. The book of Acts records the miracles that were performed by them. One instance in Acts chapter 9 (32-43), Peter was on a visit to Lydda and Joppa, where he performed two miracles by healing the lame and raising the dead. In Lydda, a man called Aeneas was bedridden for eight years. Peter prayed for him and immediately he began to walk. After this miracle, the believers in Joppa heard Peter was nearby and sent for him. They wanted him to pray for a woman named Tabitha, who fell ill and recently died. Once he got there, he prayed for her and immediately, she woke up. Peter's prayer for these two people was able to cause miraculous changes in their lives.

Acts chapter 16 recorded an occasion where Paul and Silas were arrested and thrown in prison, because they had set a young girl free from the Spirit of divination. In the middle of the night both of them began to pray and worship while other prisoners were listening. When suddenly there was an earthquake that shook the foundations of the prison. The prison doors were opened and all the chains of the prisoners were loosed. It was the power of prayer and worship that set them and all the other prisoners free.

2nd Corinthians 10:4a We use God's mighty weapons, not worldly weapons,

Prayer and worship are powerful weapons of our warfare that we have as believers to make manifest the kingdom of God. When we pray in the name of Jesus, we receive answers that cause miraculous changes in our lives and that of others. Our worship is pleasing to God and causes him to release an abundance of blessings upon us. Paul, Peter and Silas were men filled with the Holy Spirit and had the authority of Jesus. We are also are Spirit- filled beings and have the same authority of Christ. Let us engage more in prayer and worship to God as powerful weapons in our warfare. With our divine authority we are able to live supernatural Christian lives while on our *Journey to the vineyard.*

Chapter Thirteen
Go tell it on the mountain

Born in the 1990's and growing up in Lagos as a child was so much fun. During the Christmas break, my parents would take I and my sisters to my Grandma's house in Surulere. It was a very big house with five bedrooms, which was also where my late mum and all her siblings grew up. Some of my cousins already lived in the same building in another flat. My aunt also would bring her kids and we all did spend the Christmas together. On Christmas eve, we would all walk to the Church for the midnight mass. It was quite frightening walking down the streets at that late hour, because of the fire knockouts. These were not the same as the sky fireworks and were quite dangerous. There were several stories of people who usually suffered burns as a result. Anyway, we did our best to avoid them and get safely to church.

On Christmas morning, when we had all rested from the Mass which usually closed around 1.am, everyone would gather at the backyard of the house. It was time for family cooking! We often made a variety of Christmas meals which included jollof rice, fried rice, assorted chicken stew, barbecue, moin moin (traditional beans pudding), egusi soup and pounded yam. Once the food was ready, Grandma would serve them into fancy glass dishes and put them in baskets ready for distribution. It was our family tradition to share food to the neighbours on Christmas day. This was also quite popular amongst many Lagosians in the 1990's, because we always did receive lots of food baskets from other neighbours.

By afternoon, we were all dressed in our new Christmas clothes and ready to go. I didn't quite like the Christmas dress as it was the standard 1990's girls big dress with a belt tied to the back (*mama tie me belt* - as we fondly called it). Anyway, there was always a long list of families we were to hand the baskets. We also took with us Christmas cards which was written on them the *Good will message on the birth of Jesus Christ*. We often paired ourselves in twos to distribute the baskets and wished everyone merry Christmas as we went along. By evening we were exhausted and got back home to have our own Christmas meal. We had fulfilled our mission to *Go tell it on the mountain.*

The song *Go tell it on the mountain* sang by most people during Christmas reminds us of our mission to announce the good news of Christ. It is not for the 1990's kids alone but for every believer to preach the message of the Gospel. Most Christmas celebrations are quite grand with lots of decorations everywhere, but still many people do not know what the celebration is about. On Christmas eve, it is common to see parties celebrated to mark the season. Some people see it as only a form of seasonal holiday and do not receive the actual message of the birth of Christ.

Makes me wonder; how do we get people to know Christ?, If we only wait till December 25th to post on our Whatsapp status; *Jesus is the reason for the season.* While it is a good time to remind people of the reason for celebration and also spend our time with them just as we love to. Will it make a difference if we spoke to people more often about the birth of Jesus? Will it make a difference if we don't leave this message for only the Christmas season?

Matthew 28 :19 a Go therefore and make disciples of all the nations...

Preaching the Gospel is not only for ordained Pastors or church leaders as some people might think. It is for every believer who has had an encounter with Christ. Once you have met him, you are entitled to talk about him. There are several instances in the bible where people encountered Christ and went about announcing the Good news. One instance accounted for in Mark Chapter one was when Jesus healed a man with leprosy.

Jesus instructed him not to tell anyone , but go straight to the priest for examination. The man could not hold back his excitement, but went about proclaiming his testimony to everyone. It was too good to be true; no one had been able to heal him from his leprosy. He had only just met Jesus and received his instant healing. This wasn't a testimony anyone could have held back. He was made whole by Jesus and wanted everyone to meet the person who had healed him from his disease. As a result a large number of people surrounded Jesus because they also wanted to know him; the man who can heal people from their diseases. We can tell others about our testimony so that others may come to know Christ.

2nd Corinthians 5: 18 Now all things are of God, who has reconciled us to Himself through Jesus Christ, and has given us the ministry of reconciliation.

We have all being given the ministry of reconciliation and there is no better way to reconcile people to Christ than to tell them about him. Most work places have rules that do not allow people to engage in religious conversations. Being that a lot of young adults, youths and teenagers are very conversant with the use of technology, we can engage in social media envagelism.

Most young people these days involve in idolatry. by focusing all their time on celebrity lifestyle, wealth and fashion. Some suffer from low self esteem or other psychological issues as a result of media bullying. It is important that we do not conform to worldly standards or engage in time wasting conversations that might affect one's psychological health. We need to use social media as a Godly tool for networking with others. Your Instagram, TikTok, Face book, Twitter page, You Tube or other social media platforms should speak the message of Christ. Decency and moderation is also key for every young believer. It is not a place to show off wealth or social status, but a place to show off Christ so that others may come to know him. Let us also keep in mind that we are the *brides of Christ* and need to be moderate in our dressing.

'Matthew 25 : 29 For to everyone who has, more will be given, and he will have abundance; but from him who does not have, even what he has will be taken away

As ambassadors for Christ, we are called to represent him with our God given talents, gifts and skills. Sadly, many young people seem to have sold their talents for worldly pleasures. The parable of the talents in Matthew 25:14 -30 reminds us of what our Journey to the vineyard is like. On the last day we will all account for our investment in God's vineyard. Jesus assures us that we will have an abundance, if we are productive with our God given talents. Anyone who invests their talent(s) wisely will be given even more and those who do not use it wisely will have it taken away. Hence, whether you are a singer, dancer, actor, writer. artist, presenter, endeavour to utilise your talents, gifts and skills in God's vineyard. Ask the Holy Spirit for guidance to enable you invest wisely while on your Journey to the Vineyard.

Chapter Fourteen
Workers in the vineyard

I seldom buy fruits because I hardly ever remember to eat them and they go rotten. Even though I tried a few times to incorporate them into my diet, that hasn't seemed to work quite well for me. I am not someone to go with routines, especially when it comes to dietary plans. I prefer the flexibility of just waking up to plan out what to cook based on what is available in the fridge or food cupboard.

Do I ever get to eat fruits? Perhaps when I find them in the staff room. My colleagues at work often buy grape fruits and this is the best time I could pack a handful and just munch. I could go on and on munching them till the whole box is finished. I can't just seem to get enough of them, especially the blue black grapes. They are really very tasty and succulent. I am certain the workers in the grape *Vineyard* must have put in a lot of effort to ensure that these precious fruits are well harvested.

Matthew 20: 16b NKJV For many are called, but few chosen."

God's vineyard certainly does need a lot of diligent workers to ensure that there is fruitfulness. Just like the grape vineyard, workers need to invest their time, skills and labour wisely to produce a successful harvest. The parable of the workers in the vineyard (Matthew 20: 1-16) reminds us that many of us are called to be workers in God's vineyard, but only a few are chosen. We are called to a life of service to God and are also required to serve others faithfully. To ensure productivity, we should endeavour to collaborate with other workers in the vineyard alike. It doesn't matter who was there before you or who got in after you. What is required of each and everyone of us is our commitment to service.

1ˢᵗ Corinthians 12: 7 A spiritual gift is given to each of us so we can help each other.

As believers we have been blessed with Spiritual gifts for the edification of the body of Christ. We are many parts but one body of Christ and none of us can function without the other. These gifts have been given to us to build our faith and for us to function together as one. 1st Corinthians chapter 12 lists out the Spiritual gifts that we have been blessed with. Though, there are several other spiritual gifts that we receive from the Holy Spirit as we walk closely with him. For instance, some people are gifted as intercessors and are able to intercede for others in prayers, while Some are endowed with the gift of encouragement and are able to counsel others. There are also various divine callings listed out in the same chapter such as Apostles, Prophets, teachers, leaders. All of this is to ensure that there is Spiritual maturity amongst believers and we are able to call others into the body of Christ.

Take for instance, in our usual Church services, there are workers who commit their time to ensuring the service is well organised. Our service is set aside to honour God and to fellowship with other brethren. It is quite obvious that a lot of work is put into the service. The church building for example has to be clean and tidy with the chairs well arranged. There has to be decorations on the altar with good lighting. Ushers have to come early enough to coordinate the service. We are being led into worship by the Choristers who must have committed their time to rehearsal. There are the drummers, pianist, technical team and so many other people who come together to ensure that we can gather to worship God.

We are reminded that no spiritual gift or calling is less valuable than the other and God has called us together for a divine purpose. It is important for us to build each other up, ensuring that no one is neglected. Just as we take care of our body and not neglect any part, so we are to take care of each other as one body of Christ. For us to productively work in harmony, we must emulate Christ who is the Head of the Church. He is the author and finisher of our faith and our service to God must honour him.

Chapter Fifteen
A bountiful Harvest

Stand in the rain as the clouds go grey

The thunder roars and the earth sings

The season's just beginning

The sunlight it hides as the clouds make way

For the pouring of my blessings

I will not be afraid

see it now, I understand, I know

So I embrace it

Dance in the rain it's for my seeds to grow

For every prayer and every seed I've sown

The Lord of the harvest knows

I'm reaping back a hundred fold

The land is green - it's green

Ooooh

The land is green - it's green

Can't you see?

The harvest is ready

Cos the Lord of the harvest told me so

It's green - it's green for me
It's green - it's green for me

Are you a worker in God's vineyard? The Harvest is ripe! The Harvest is ready! Listening to TY Bello's song *The land is green* when I was younger didn't make much meaning to me as it does now. I would just dance to the song and enjoy the music. Not until recently did I realise that the lyrics are scriptural. Our journey to the vineyard is one of planting and harvesting.

The song refers to a person who has sown seeds in the past and was waiting for their seeds to grow. At the time of planting they were not certain of the outcome of their harvest. At first they were discouraged by the seasons that came in form of thunder and rain. They would have preferred if the Sun was still Shining - perhaps they thought this might have been appropriate for the season. Towards the end, they begin to appreciate the rain, realising that it was necessary for the soil to be watered. They were no longer afraid of the rainy season as they were initially, but joyfully awaited their bountiful harvest. They are delighted by the words the *Lord of the Harvest* revealed to them. In the end they are glad they waited as they could now see the fruits of their labour, *It is a bountiful harvest!*

Ecclesiastes 3:1 For everything there is a season, a time for every activity under heaven

In Ecclesiastes chapter three, the writer reminds us that there are times and seasons of life. There will be a time when all that we have planted in God's vineyard will yield results. We are encouraged to have an eternal mindset, even as we wait. It is not a time to be weary but to rejoice in our hope of Eternal salvation. The benefits of times and seasons is that we mature in the process and for each phase we reap a bountiful harvest. Walking closely with God and seeking his counsel helps us understand the different phases of life we might encounter and what is required of us.

For instance, someone who is earnestly praying for a promotion at work is expected to equip themselves for the role by taking professional courses. If they failed to do so, they might not qualify for the promotion and the role would be given to another who was well prepared. If God has given you a vision that you will be a great singer, you need to work closely with him for that promise to be fulfilled. Your waiting period is a time for faithful prayers and practical investment. Just sitting at home and waiting for the day you will be that great singer might not happen if you do not make any investments with your singing talent. While praying, you can start writing out your songs, take online music classes, enrol in the vocal lessons or join the choir. Above all of this, God makes everything beautiful in his own time.

Matthew 9: 37 "The harvest is great, but the workers are few.

Still not a worker in God's vineyard?. It is not too late to make that decision to clock in. The Lord of the harvest awaits you and is ever ready to receive you. Simply say *Yes* to him. There is a numerous call for workers in the vineyard and *God will equip you with all you need for doing his* will (Hebrews 13:21). There's a calling to be a Pastor, Singer, Worship leader, Actor, Dancer, Drummer, Instrumentalist, Writer, Pod caster, Presenter, Counsellor, Intercessor, Apostle, Prophet and so much more. We have been empowered by the Holy Spirit to *harvest Souls for God's kingdom, deliver people from captivity and oppression and restore sight to the blind (Luke 4:19). This is the Spiritual harvest that should matter to us the most.* There is a *lost one* out there who will be restored by your Gospel music, dance or drama. There is a *broken hearted* person who needs to hear your words of encouragement. There is an *addict* who needs your prayers to be set free from captivity. There is so much greatness inside of you that the world is waiting to experience. God has empowered you to uplift you, so you can uplift others. *use it so you don't lose it.*

Printed in Great Britain
by Amazon

22136752R00057